SEVEN WAYS TO COMMUNICATE WITH ANGELIC BEINGS

ARE YOUR
Angels
TALKING
TO YOU?

Diego Berman PhD

ARE YOUR

Angels

TALKING

TO YOU?

ARE YOUR

Angels

TALKING

TO YOU?

**SEVEN WAYS TO COMMUNICATE
WITH ANGELIC BEINGS**

℘

Diego Berman PhD

Author of

<u>'My Divine Connection:
Fifty Steps to Your Divine Fulfillment
on Earth'</u>

To the Divine Angels

CONTENTS

INTRODUCTION

We shall find Peace,
we shall hear Angels,
we shall see the Sky
sparkling with diamonds.
—Anton Chekhov
(Russian writer, 1860-1904)

The presence of Angels in human life has been well documented since the early days of our human civilization. From ancient stories in sacred texts to modern personal encounters, Angels have been shaping the lives of millions of people throughout our history on this planet.

Angels, or Angelic Beings, are non-physical entities whose energy vibrate at frequencies much higher than our physical bodies and the physical world around us.

Angels can be found everywhere in the Universe, and there is definitely no shortage of them. Angelic Beings are being constantly created by the same all-encompassing energy Source that supports us humans and all of the creations in the Universe. People refer to this Divine energy source as God, the Divine, All That Is, Universe, the Creator, etc. Therefore, the Angels and us share a Divine connection at a deep level.

Although frequently associated with the main religious world faiths, Angels are non-denominational beings and their presence, guidance, and unconditional love is accessible to all human beings equally.

Why do Angels exist? Why do humans exist? These are difficult questions to answer, but one thing is clear: Angels are a natural aspect of our human Divine Connection.

Several books have been written on the nature of Angels and the plethora of roles they play in our human lives. In this book, I will broadly use the terms 'Angels' and 'Angelic Beings' to refer to all the several different 'categories' of Angelic Beings such as Archangels, guardian Angels, healing Angels, and others. Terminology aside, the key common denominator that emerges from all these different Angels-Humans interactions is *Communication*.

Angels are one of the main communication channels by which the Divine sends its messages to us. Angelic Beings are Divine messengers par excellence. Angels act like 'communication bridges', or 'divine postmen', carrying and delivering messages and prayers between the pure energy of the Divine and our human experience on the physical plane.

The answer then to the question 'Are Angels talking to you?' is a big YES.

Whether you feel their presence or not, Angels are around you and everyone at all times, including right now as you read these words. They are here with us to assist us in our physical experience on Earth, what we call life. The Angels' intention for each of us is that we live a joyful, healthy, loving, and meaningful life.

Receiving and understanding your Angels' messages can assist you in several ways, from assistance in day-to-day simple decision-making to encouragement and support in big life-changing situations.

That said, Angels do not interfere or intervene directly in our lives, they respect our free will. Unless there is a critical situation that might put our life in danger, Angels want us to reach out to them, to open our hearts and minds to their loving Divine presence in our lives. They are basically waiting for us to dial into their angelic Divine frequency.

From the very first moment you start connecting with the Angels, they will be talking back to you. Angels will choose one or several ways to deliver their messages to you.

Make no mistake, once you ask for Angelic assistance, the Angels will try over and over to send their message to you across the vibrational continuum of reality. Remember, Angels are non-physical beings, and their non-physical messages need to reach you here on the physical dimensions!

How do the messages of the Angels find their way to you? I will get a bit 'technical' here.

Each of us carries a unique energy 'fingerprint' that identifies us at the vibrational level. This energetic pattern is shaped by a combination of a large number of factors including your Soul history and experience, your human history, your ancestral energy patterns, your daily meditation and self-caring practices, and many others. This unique personal vibrational pattern together with the strength of your **Divine Connection*** will shape your preferred way, or style, to tune into the Angels' frequencies and their messages.

In the next section of this book, you will learn seven of the Angels' main preferred ways to send their messages across to you.

Before we move on, let's take a moment to relax your mind and body. Sit in a comfortable position, close your eyes, take a couple of deep breaths, and call upon your Angels to surround you with their unconditional Love and Wisdom, to help you clearly identify their preferred way to communicate with you. You can say the following affirmation, either silently or aloud, to start attuning your energy to the energy of the Angels:

"Dear Angels, I call upon you now, please surround me with your Divine Love and Light, and help me clearly receive and understand the Divine Guidance you have for me. Thank you. Thank you. Thank you."

* * *

As you read through the seven different modes of Angelic communication pay attention to any feelings or insights you might receive. You might find that your Angels are using more than one communication channel!

Identifying and understanding your preferred style of Angelic communication will allow you to receive the Angels' messages more frequently and in a crystal-clear way. But more importantly, their messages and guidance will assist you in co-creating a life of purpose, health, peace, and joy, in partnership with the Divine.

*You can discover and strengthen your unique personal connection with the Divine by reading and working with my recently released book 'MY DIVINE CONNECTION: FIFTY STEPS TO YOUR DIVINE FULFILLMENT ON EARTH'. Get your copy on Amazon by clicking here.

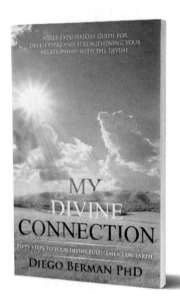

Visit www.mydivineconnectionsite.wordpress.com
to subscribe to Diego's Readers Group and to stay up to date
with new FREE GIFTS, book promotions, and Angel
Readings discounts.

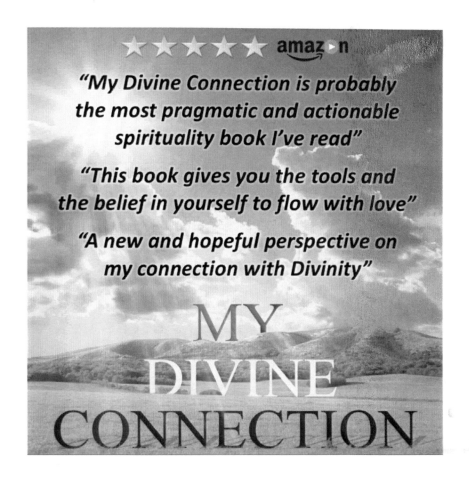

THE SEVEN ANGELIC COMMUNICATION CHANNELS

These seven modes of Angelic communication establish the foundation for your communication with the Divine. As you continue developing your Divine Connection and your relationship with the Angels deepens, you will find that you will become an 'expert' in one, or more, of these Angelic communication channels. In time, your energy will most likely be attuned to a preferred 'Angel-sense' or communication style.

My first encounter with an Angel (Archangel Raphael) took me by surprise. I had no prior experience with working with Angels when this event took place, yet, this Angel found a way to communicate with me. As I was sending energy to a client during a distant healing session, I heard a deep voice on my left ear saying: "I am Archangel Raphael, and I am here to assist you in your healing arts". From that moment on, this Angel has been teaching me and supporting my work.

This is a clear example of the first Angelic communication channel as you will see below.

Let's now look at these amazing ways of Angelic communication and start receiving the Angels' messages!

Angelic communication channel 1: The Voices of Angels

Not everyone 'hears' angelic voices as a real audible sound. But if you do, it means you are using an extrasensory channel called 'clairaudience', meaning clear hearing. You are basically hearing with your mind's ears.

The Angels' voices sound different than your own voice. They can sound soothing, be deep or mellow, and one feels as if their voices are coming from an area outside of your head. For example, every time I connect with Archangel Raphael his voice appears to be located on the frontal-left side of my body.

Different Angels emit different energy frequencies, so their voices will be translated differently once it reaches you. Sometimes the voice is faint and soft, and other times it can be commanding and strong, depending on the situation you find yourself in.

You might hear their voices while you meditate, sleep, work, or are involved in a creative process. Another auditory way in which the Angels make their presence known to you is through music. Hearing celestial music, such as a choir or a chamber music melody, is a way for the Angels to say "We are here with you, remember you are never alone".

Other times, Angels like to catch our attention by triggering high-frequency tones in our ears. (Please do not confuse this with the physical symptom called 'tinnitus').

If this is your preferred Angelic communication channel, you might be hearing their messages right now! Are your Angels talking to you?...

Angelic communication channel 2: Seeing the Angels

Most people want to see Angels. As humans, we heavily rely daily on our physical visual system. We are seeing beings. But the energy of Angels is much higher than the visible frequencies our physical eyes can see. That said, there are stories in which Angels take physical form in times of extreme human distress to intervene directly on the physical planes.

Most of us are able see Angels in our mind's eyes. This extrasensory channel is called 'clairvoyance', clear seeing. You might be able to 'see' energies of different colors when you connect with your Angels. These images appear superimposed on what your physical eyes are seeing, however this might require some practice to achieve.

That said, the important issue here is that you 'see' the messages your Angels are sending you. If clairvoyance is your preferred communication channel, you might receive angelic messages in the form of a picture, or a short movie, in your mind's eyes when you ask for Angelic guidance. It will be helpful in this case to close your physical eyes to reduce the interference coming from the physical world.

The dream state is a wonderful time for Angels to imprint their messages visually. Simply call upon them right before going to bed, with the clear intention to relax your mind and allow their messages to reach you in your dreams.

If clairvoyance is your preferred Angelic communication channel, you might be seeing your Angels' messages right now! Are your Angels talking to you?...

Angelic communication channel 3: The Touch of Angels

Do you sometimes get feelings or body responses completely out of the blue, especially when you are exposed to new situations or thinking about a particular person? Sometimes we call this intuition, or 'gut feeling'. Our physical bodies can act like amazing walking antennas constantly receiving physical and non-physical stimuli.

Angels know of our physical sensitivity, and can take advantage of this style of communication to send their messages to us. This extrasensory channel is called 'clairsentience', or clear feeling. When you ask your Angels for guidance on a particular issue you will feel parts of your body react to their messages by using your clairsentience. For example, you might feel your stomach slightly tighten, or develop goosebumps, or you might experience a warm, or cold, feeling in specific areas of your body. All these are physical manifestations of the Angels' energy and messages on your own body.

Sometimes you might even feel a brush of air on your face without any windows or doors open nearby. These are your Angels talking to you directly to and through your physical body!

If this is your preferred Angelic communication channel, you might be feeling their messages right now! Are your Angels talking to you?...

Angelic communication channel 4: You Simply Know Your Angels

This is an Angelic communication channel that is somewhat difficult to explain, simply because when you receive a message from your Angels through this mode of communication you just 'know' it! There is no delay, no need for physical signs, no need for images or words for you to understand the message. You just get an immediate 'angelic download' into your energy system.

The Angels love to send us these type of 'lightening' messages when our mind is relaxed and more receptive to non-physical messages. This could happen while we are sleeping, daydreaming, creating, and even while showering or walking. These are activities in which our mind tends to wander is not fully focused on physical reality.

This Angelic communication mode is responsible for those 'aha!' and 'eureka!' moments, in which we seem to suddenly see or know something that we didn't know before.

When Angels send you messages this way, it feels like there is no lag between the moment you ask your question and the moment you receive their message. It truly feels like a real telepathic conversation is taking place between you and the Angels.

This extrasensory channel is called 'claircognizance', or clear knowing, in which the Angels directly tune the frequency of their message to that of your own mind.

If this is your preferred Angelic communication channel, you might already know the message the Angels have for you right now! Are your Angels talking to you?...

Angelic communication channel 5: The Fragrances of Angels

This communication channel is less common than those we have covered so far, but it does occur in some people. This particular extrasensory channel used by the Angels to deliver their messages to you is called 'clairscent' or 'clairolfaction', meaning clear smelling.

This is a rather limited way of communication, since it is restricted to certain fragrances or scents you are familiar with. Sometimes, as we ask for Angelic guidance on a particular situation we suddenly smell a puff of aroma out of the blue. This scent could be reminiscent of flowers, fruits, trees, or even less appealing odors.

Your Angels are connecting directly to you 'mind's nose', energetically speaking of course. Needless to say, in these situations the source of the fragrance is not found near you in the physical world.

Your Angels know you very well, and they know you will associate a particular scent to a memory or feeling. It is this powerful personal association of smell and memory that will help you understand and translate the messages your Angels are sending you. The appearance of a pleasant fragrance will indicate a positive and encouraging sign from your Angels, while unpleasant odors would indicate a less positive or a 'watch-your-steps-carefully-here' type of message.

If this is your preferred Angelic communication channel, you might be already smelling some of their messages right now! Are your Angels talking to you?...

Angelic communication channel 6: Letters From Your Angels

This Angelic communication channel is a direct partnership between your Angels and your writing and motor skills. Many people call this practice 'intuitive writing' or 'automatic writing'.

This is the process in which you sit with a pen and paper (or a computer), ask a question to your Angels, and then your hands and fingers seem to receive the message directly, seemingly bypassing your conscious mind. It is as if your Angels are dictating you a letter from Above.

You might call this extrasensory channel 'claireloquence', or clear expression. Creative people and artists usually have a well-developed sense of claireloquence. You can develop this communication channel by writing on a journal on a daily basis, and asking questions to your Angels as you write. You will be surprised to see what happens!

This type of communication is quite useful when the Angels want to send you supportive and empowering messages, as their message becomes imprinted on a physical object (the paper or the computer screen). This way, you can always go back and read these messages over and over again.

If this is your preferred Angelic communication channel, you might already be feeling the need to grab a piece of paper and start writing away! Are your Angels talking to you?...

Angelic communication channel 7: Channeling Your Angels

On this final Angelic communication channel, *you* become the channel itself.

As we continually work on our personal growth and development by letting go of the emotional weights that keep us anchored to pain and suffering, we increase our energy vibrations and slowly ascend and access higher frequencies of energy manifestation. It is in this state that we can become clear communication channels of the Divine and the Angels.

Directly channeling the Angels' messages feels like connecting to a consciousness stream, in which the Angels' energy flows to you and through you effortlessly. You and the Angels become one, which in spiritual truth, we always are.

As I mentioned before, this level of channeling occurs when our own energy vibrations are high enough for the Angels to directly tap into it. This type of Angelic communication involves all of the previous six channels and many others that are beyond the scope of this book.

Channeling your Angels requires a constant work on ourselves. This process involves taking care of your diet, physical body, emotional balance, and spiritual practice. Channeling your Angels is truly a lifestyle.

If this is your preferred Angelic communication channel, you are most likely able to experience the Angels' energy and their messages as if you are One with them. Are your Angels talking to you?...

AFTERWORD

It is my hope that this book has helped you discover and understand your preferred way to connect and interact with your loving Angels. The Angelic Beings are here to assist you in enacting the Divine plan that your Soul has chosen to express at this time on this physical plane. The Angels are your Divine friends, your life coaches, and your Divine healers. All you have to do is call upon them and develop your personal relationship with their Divine essence.

The seven communication channels described in this book form the basis of your Divine communication. That said, your Angels and other Divine Guides and Teachers can also use other ways to communicate with you. These 'signs from Heaven' can appear in your outer physical world, as opposed to your inner extrasensory world described in this book.

Heaven and your Angels might try to catch your attention by sending you different types of signals. These could range from seeing repetitive numbers, experiencing synchronistic events, finding feathers and coins, or seeing butterflies, rainbows, and other sky-related signs. I will be describing these 'external signs' from the Divine and your Angels in a future book.

Your Angels are indeed talking to you. The question now is: How will you be listening?...

Much love and blessings.

Diego.

ABOUT THE AUTHOR

Since early childhood, **Dr. Diego Berman** was interested in experiences that challenge the mainstream paradigms. He grew up in Buenos Aires, Argentina, where he obtained his first degree in Biology and Molecular Genetics at the University of Buenos Aires. Later he developed an interest in the brain and cognitive functions, which led him to move to Israel and pursue a Ph.D. in Neuroscience at the Weizmann Institute of Science. In 2002, Diego moved to New York City and continued his scientific work at Columbia University as an Assistant Professor, focusing on the neurobiology of Alzheimer's disease. In parallel to his academic and scientific career, Diego's personal inner journey led him into the fields of consciousness studies, Buddhist meditation, yoga, and other paths of inner contemplative practices. In 2010, Diego's first encounter with Archangel Raphael was featured in Doreen Virtue's book 'The Healing Miracles of Archangel Raphael'. Diego is a certified Nutri-Energetic Systems© practitioner, an Assertiveness Life Coach©, and an Angel Card Reader©. Diego also speaks Light Languages, which is yet another form of vibrational energy balancing. In early 2017, Diego published his first spiritual book called 'My Divine Connection: Fifty Steps to Your Divine Fulfillment on Earth'.

You can find Diego on his Facebook page at:

www.facebook.com/FindYourTrueNorth

Tools for a Joyful and Purposeful Living

Visit www.mydivineconnectionsite.wordpress.com

to subscribe to Diego's Readers Group and stay up to date with free gifts, new book promotions,

and Angel Readings discounts.

If you found this book informative and helpful, I'd truly appreciate it if you could leave a short review on Amazon. Thank you!

Manufactured by Amazon.ca
Acheson, AB